America is on Trial!

by

Robert G. Butler

Dedications

This is dedicated my children and grandchildren. They are my legacy to this world.

I also dedicate this comprehensive document to all patriotic, decent Americans who I trust to do the right thing this election year.

Food for Thought:

Time for the New Age of Reason! "He who will not reason is a bigot; he who cannot is a fool; and he who dares not is a slave." (William Drummond: Academical Questions)

"One ought, every day at least, to hear a little song, read a good poem, see a fine picture, and, if it were possible, to speak a few reasonable words." (Johann Wolfgang Von Goethe: Wilhelm Meister's Apprenticeship.)

Reason is "the power of comprehending, inferring, or thinking especially in orderly rational ways." https://www.merriam-webster.com/dictionary/reason)

Reason means that our elected officials seek all sides to questions, debate openly and honestly, looking for solutions and laws which improve life, advance science and technology, ensure that education works for everyone, and protect not only the people's lives but also the environment, whatever the cost. Only people of reason can do this; those who seek to advance only their own interests or those of special interest groups have no place in leadership. One of the things which separates humans from other animals or life forms is the ability to REASON. However, unless you are willing to examine other points of view, the facts and REASONING and logic behind those viewpoints, you are not exercising the ability to REASON! "Men (and women) who are governed by reason...desire for themselves nothing which they do not also desire for the rest of mankind." (Benedict Spinoza: Ethics, 1667

It is the component which the members of a democratic political society must possess in order to not be oppressed by a demagogue, a dictator, or a monarchy. The United States has long depended on those who have been empowered to govern, to lead through the power of reason, to search for truth and to avoid those who would attempt to influence laws and policies which are not in the best interests of a super majority of citizens.

We, the citizens, the voters, must demand more from those who we allow to run for office and especially from those that we ultimately elect. When Congress passes bills that support only a minority of citizens or special interest groups, they do not serve the best interests of all Americans. That should be unacceptable! Any bill that is passed should be supported by at least 60% of House members.

When judges are appointed to life terms by only a single vote, that is not in the best interest of all Americans. Anyone appointed for life should be acceptable to at least 60% of Senators.

Being elected to office should end a public servant's association with a particular political party.

These men and women represent ALL AMERICANS and owe their loyalty ONLY TO THEM and the U.S. CONSTITUTION!

We have reached a dangerous point in our "experiment in freedom" here in the United States. There are those who wish to push their religious or personal beliefs on all Americans. The proper way to complain in this democracy is through editorials, peaceful marches in the streets, and either running for office or peacefully supporting the candidates of choice VIOLENCE IS NEVER ACCEPTABLE! Neither is bullying, lying, cheating, intimidation, or discrimination!

The U.S. Constitution is not perfect and can be amended if such a proposition can make it through the process set down for such a change. Our rights are defined by that document.

Prologue

This is the moment for America to move out of this darkest chapter in American history which began with the assassination of President John F. Kennedy. It was followed by the misguided years of the Vietnam War that was ended by President Nixon, who promptly dropped the Presidency into shame with the Watergate scandal, which was followed not too many years afterward with the "Savings & Loan" and "Hostages for weapons" administration of an otherwise fine President Ronald Reagan. Not too many years later, the country was embarrassed by the shameful actions of President Bill Clinton who impeached but not removed from office. He should have resigned and would have if he'd had the character that a President should really have. He was followed by an inept President who, instead of putting the full assets of the F.B.I. and C.I.A. at work investigating what really happened and who was responsible for the attack on America on September 11, 2001, he lied to the American public and convinced Congress to attack Iraq, which led us to the quagmire that exists in the Middle East today. President Obama misled the American public, telling them that "they could keep their current doctor and insurance" as the Affordable Care Act was passed. It has turned out to be a program with many good qualities, but it was rammed through Congress before it was ready.

It is because of these lies that Congress turned into the truly partisan mess that it is at present. Government became so mistrusted, along with the politicians stagnating in Washington, that enough American voters decided to put in a TV celebrity whose only goal was to "win" and celebrate the demolition of America's reputation with its allies as he has refused to do anything/say anything that would anger Russian President Putin, who led an attack on American democracy during the 2016 campaign and is continuing to sew discord among Americans.

We need a "leader," someone who cares only about the best interests of the American public, nothing else! The United States now has a chance to elect someone who only cares about the citizens of this country, someone who has nothing to gain personally except a salary. It is time for American voters to "hire" a leader, not buy another politician. A great America leader is someone who will surround him/herself with qualified, experienced people to write the legislation and walk it through the dark corridors of Congress until it returns to the President's desk for signature.

It's not the President's job to write laws! It's the President' job to LEAD, provide guidance, set standards and policy, work in unison with the elected Congress to make sure this country is safe, protect its citizens from fraud, scams, and injustice, and use the wealth of the country for the benefit of all. We must rebuild old bridges, improve highways, protect our electrical grid from the eventual damage of solar flares or cyber attacks, fund and encourage the creation of new, cleaner methods of electrical generation using geothermal, solar, water/wind turbines, etc., and expand our manufacturing capabilities to replace foreign dependence with jobs here at home.

Part of the reason that technology leapt forward in the 1960's to what we have today was the space program. I believe that our destiny lies not by continuing to exist on this planet but by colonizing and mining other planets, both within our solar system and elsewhere. One day, hopefully thousands of years into the future, our sun will die out (or we will completely poison this planet) and life itself will cease to exist on Earth. There are visionaries who are already looking to that future, but the United States, along with those around the world with the same vision, must lead, not sit by and watch.

The people of the United States and this planet face serious dangers and must work together to solve them. Nuclear weapons, terrorism, poverty, crime and criminal enterprises, climate issues, meteors, asteroids, solar flares, etc. We must find a way to work together to survive and thrive. We cannot allow political or religious or economic differences to drive us apart. There are always solutions to problems; people simply have to be willing and able to work together, find compromises which allow for differences.

We all live on this planet and MUST share its resources. The greatest assets are the human brain and the human heart. Leadership is what is missing from our country right now. A leader brings together the best and is the facilitator! I don't have all the answers, but the following chapters will lay out a comprehensive list of challenges that we face, along with a solid plan for changing the political and economic reality in the United States, with a few ideas of how to reduce the tensions and dangers around the world. We have to see what should be done and can be done, NOT what hasn't been done.

Placing blame on the past keeps us trapped in the quagmire of insults/personal defense! I believe that this country needs someone "neutral" enough to have an administration made up of members from Democratic, Republican, Independent, and Libertarian parties.

The most important non-governmental partner/resource is "investigative journalism." That doesn't mean accusing people or spreading lies. Real, honest journalism should provide a welcome oversight for everyone in public service. Elected officials have nothing to fear from the truth, do they? It is imperative that public servants be held accountable, be held to a higher standard because the public trust is the basis for any government of the people, by the people, and FOR THE PEOPLE!

Anyone who works for the American people in any administration cannot be allowed to abuse the public trust, waste taxpayer money, or be above the law. Elected officials WILL make mistakes, of course, but nothing should be hidden. American voters can forgive honest mistakes; they will never forgive intentional lying, cheating, or theft. Every American's philosophy should be that, regardless of the party affiliation of a candidate for office or a person who accepts a position working within the federal government, once that person takes that position, he/she must no longer have a party affiliation.

When a person becomes President or Congressional member or a member of the Judiciary or any appointee, the only loyalty lies with the American People, PERIOD! We must all work for the "best interests" of all citizens, not the interests of any party or special interest group or other affiliation. It cannot be any other way!

Immigration Reform/NOT AMNESTY/Border Security!

The current controversy over illegal immigrants can and should be dealt with in a more humane, beneficial manner if we use a smarter approach. Sending millions of people out of the country would create a "worker/business/job" gap that would be irresponsible. Building an expensive, mostly **ineffective "wall"** that has been promoted, is both a waste of money and a waste of time. Destroying the lives of the "DACA" kids by shipping them overseas to countries of their birth but where they have almost never lived is heartless and a waste of potentially highly productive, grateful future taxpayers and citizens! There is a better way, and everyone wins!

A. Convicted felons (except those convicted of murder or who are major drug dealers) and "gang affiliated" non-citizens must be deported immediately. IF they return to the United States and are recaptured (since they would be told that they could never again set foot on American soil), they would be subject to "life" sentences in federal prisons, new ones designed specifically to house such prisoners in single occupant cells, though humanely treated. They would be able to see and interact with other prisoners but have no physical contact, which should be the model for all future prisons.

B. All other "undocumented" non-citizens should be given six months (or a reasonable period) to come forward to register for a "temporary residency permit." At that time, they will be fingerprinted, photographed, had their DNA taken, and issued a **"Photo ID-orange social security card"**(this is NOT a "green card") and be allowed to openly work legally, following all standard laws and regulations that would be expected of any "citizen worker." They could be either employees or self-employed and would file tax returns like everyone else. One difference is that holders of the "orange" cards would NOT benefit from their social security/National Health Insurance contributions. Until they become American citizens, they would not accrue those benefits; those contributions would, in effect, be part of the added cost for living and working in the United States and taking a job which would otherwise be filled by an American citizen. This would help defray social security expenditures for the rest of us. It is one of the penalties for illegally entering the country. Once they become citizens, they would begin the process of building their own social security accounts for future retirements. Their "past" salaries/wages would have no effect on their future retirement benefits. They would be eligible for basic medical care insurance (private coverage from private companies) for themselves and their dependents but only if working and paying the same National Health coverage that citizens do, though their contributions (and their employer contributions) would go to their private health insurance carriers. (This part needs more study and a compromise to be fair to both "non-citizen residents" and American citizens.)

C. To become a citizen in the future, each of these "orange card" holders would be required to fulfill the same requirements as any other applicant, except that there would also be a fine (amount to be determined by Congress) that would have to be paid before citizenship would be finalized. In addition, all criminal fines, penalties, or probation must be fulfilled before citizenship would be finalized.

D. These "orange card" holders would move to the "back of the line (list)" in terms of applying for citizenship. They just wouldn't have to physically leave the country first.

E. Anyone with a "violent" felony conviction (for which time has been served) before becoming a citizen would mean immediate deportation to the country of origin and beginning the process of "going to the back of the line" while living outside the U.S. ; other applicants with felony convictions would be considered on a case-by-case basis.

F. Those seeking "asylum" with the United States will no longer be allowed to present themselves at the various border crossings. They will be required to present themselves at any of our embassies or consulates to apply for asylum, for visas, or other requirements to enter the United States.

G. In the future, there must be a better method of monitoring (searching) incoming freight, products from all sources. Currently the primary line of defense is our borders. Every item which enters this country must be checked for contraband. If that means things move more slowly across the border, then that is the price that must be paid for our security. I'm certain that a better method/system for controlling what crosses our borders in trucks, on ships, or on planes can be developed. It is in our best interests to see that it is created!

H. To be eligible for the "orange card" status, an "illegal" must be able to prove that he/she had been residing in the United States prior to Jan. 1, 20??. "Proof" will be determined by a bi-partisan committee of House and Senate members.

I. Border Security needs to be improved, enhanced. There are many ways to do that. However, repeating myself, **"Building an expensive, most-likely ineffective "wall" that has been promoted, is both a waste of money and a waste of time."** There are other proposals that make more sense, would be less expensive, and certainly more effective. Simply sending the military to the border when it is politically expedient can be illegal or simply a gimmick. Only if we were actually invaded by a military force would it the right thing to do.

A. Years ago there was a proposal to create a new "Panama-type canal" from the San Diego, CA area to Brownsville, TX. While it would be a long canal, it would be shorter and cheaper than the Panama Canal. It would be expensive, but it would create thousands of jobs, both in the building process and in operation, which would pay for it in the long run, returning those tax dollars to the Treasury and the American taxpayer. It would also make it nearly impossible to cross the border illegally crossing the canal. Patrols on both side of the canal, along with electronic monitoring would ensure that.

B. A proposal which I made several years ago would "lease" all of the southern land (aside from the towns/cities on the border) from American companies, farmers, and ranchers from the border to as much as 10 miles north, creating a new training area for the American military. Because this area would now be Military Reservations, the U.S. forces would be able to do armed patrols along the border, creating an impenetrable zone for anyone wishing to cross illegally. There could still be "agreements" with cattle ranches to allow grazing under certain circumstances in certain designated areas at no charge since the land remains the property of the land owners. Of course, the land could also be purchased using "imminent domain" laws, but I believe that the owners would rather retain ownership. Who knows what conditions might change along the border, allowing for the "control" to be returned to citizens. While this might be expensive, it would be part of the Defense budget in the future.

Only Real, True Answer to Immigration Issue?
Though no one talks about it, the only real solution to keeping people from WANTING to come to the United States en masse is helping those countries primarily south of us transform their countries and societies into places where people WANT to live, work, and raise families! Shouldn't we start with Mexico, sit down with its leaders, and develop a "Marshall-type Plan" to re-create that country. It would partially "move the battlefield" our of the United States and into Mexico. When that battle has turned, then we, and Mexico, can help the next countries, Guatemala and Belize, then so on and so on. This won't happen overnight; it will take decades if not generations to achieve. However, if a city has a weak neighborhood, the answer is not walling off the houses there; it is renovating and rejuvenating it. The analogy works with vision and action!

Citizenship
Rights and Responsibilities

Too many "citizens" take for granted being an American citizen. Some only vote when they "feel like it" or an issue "hits home." If our nation is to live up to its creed, then EVERYONE must be part of the system, not just 60% of the those actually eligible to vote. If you can't take the time to learn the issues, examine the candidates yourself, and take the time to go out and vote, maybe you should lose that right to vote for an election cycle or two. Perhaps by suffering that penalty, more citizens will act like real citizens and vote, run for office, or work for candidates and issues. In addition, there needs to be a "clearer" definition of citizenship/rights/responsibilities.

Therefore, I do propose the following constitutional amendment:

Amendment 32: United States Citizenship and Voting Responsibility

Section 1. Any person, regardless of the soil on which born, who has at least one parent who is (was, if that parent is deceased) an American citizen, whether naturalized or not, IS a natural born American citizen and eligible for **all rights and privileges** afforded to any other American citizen AND subject to the same responsibilities of any other American citizen. **Simply being born on American soil does not make you an American citizen.**

Section 2. Any person, at least 18 years of age, regardless of the soil on which born, may become a NATURALIZED American citizen by following the criteria set down by Congress. Upon satisfying all of those requirements, a person would then be eligible for any rights and privileges, except election to the office of President of the United States, afforded to any Natural born American citizen AND subject to the same responsibilities of any Natural Citizen, including registering to vote.

Section 3. It is the responsibility of every American citizen, upon turning 18 years of age, to register with the selective service system **and register to vote**. Naturalized citizens, if over the age of 34, are not required to register for selective service. Those between 18 and 35 will, from this time forward, must be registered with the selective service system at their swearing in ceremony.

Section 4. It is the responsibility of every American citizen to vote in state and federal elections. Failure to register to vote after changing addresses and precincts, whether across state lines or not, will result in loss of voting rights for one year from the time of re-registering. Failure to vote in two consecutive state or federal general elections will result in the loss of voting rights for one year from the time of re-registering. Voting is the primary method by which a democratic society can express its opinion concerning issues of the day, who will represent it, and how change will take place to protect and promote the will of the people within that society. Freedoms are not free; voting is a small price to pay for not just the survival of that society but the improvement and advancement as well. In addition, ALL citizens must be encouraged to vote, assisted in accessing the voting booth where necessary, and not discouraged because it doesn't suit one political party or another. Voter suppression is the greatest danger to a free society! It creates dissension, distrust, and partisanship, which are the symptoms of a diseased, failing society!

National Debt
Our National Shame!

One of the most serious issues facing the United States and our economic future is the "albatross" which was primarily created in the years after the attack on 9/11. Our subsequent "wars" and wasteful spending have dug us quite a deep hole, $24 Plus Trillion. Arguing over who is at fault is pointless; it serves no purpose at this moment in history because both parties share blame. We can either gripe or fix it. It continues to grow for many reasons.

If we demand that Congress have a balanced budget, then **the next step is to "capitalize" our national debt**, just as any business does when it needs funds to expand or find new capital. We should issue "tax exempt 3% National Debt Retirement Bonds" to replace the trillions of Treasury Bills, notes, bonds, etc. which are outstanding at present. I believe that the American public and American companies would jump at the chance to help the U.S. eliminate the problem of this growing debt.

There are several benefits to doing this. **First**, it would put an end date to our "National Disgrace," the debt. These would be 20-year bonds: every year the interest would be paid, and one year of the bonds would be retired. That would be a requirement of my balanced budget amendment. **Second**, it would prevent foreign countries from holding debt over our heads during economic/diplomatic negotiations because the focus would be to eliminate "foreign owned" American debt. **Third**, we are the richest country in the world; we should not be a debtor nation. **Finally**, it would ease the economic burden that all that annual interest creates. Imagine how much we could do here at home with the funds which now go just to interest payments! There will come a day when the budget is no longer saddled with debt or interest payments.

Amendment 29: National Debt Retirement Bonds

Section 1. Congress shall authorize the Treasury Department to create and sell a fixed-date, 3% interest-bearing National Debt Retirement Bond series, using them to replace the current Treasury Bills, Notes, etc. which constitute our National Debt as owed to foreign entities or non-American citizens. The interest on said bonds will be federal tax exempt. Bonds to retire foreign debt will only be available to American citizens and American corporations. Proceeds from the sale of said bonds will first be used to pay off any Federal debt owed to foreign individuals, companies, or governments. Only then will the proceeds be used to pay off domestic debt holders.

Section 2. Bond life (for retirement of foreign held American governmental debt) will be set at a term not to exceed 20 years. Each year, the national budget shall include payments such that 1/20the of the bonds are paid off (retired). The accumulated interest on the debt for 12 twelve months shall also be paid off. This shall be the second item on the President's budget, second only to the National Disaster/Emergency Trust Fund payment.

Section 3. Failure of the President or Congress to meet the terms of this amendment and fully retire the foreign national debt within the 20 year life of said bonds will be grounds for impeachment. House members could also be removed from office for said offense by a 2/3rds vote of House members.

Section 4: With the passage of this amendment, it will be illegal for foreign entities to hold American debt.

A bonus of this program will allow us to do away with the "debt ceiling" problem that has caused government shutdowns and political turmoil. We should eliminate the debt ceiling when we pass the Balanced Budget Amendment.

America MUST
"Live Within her Means"

For too long, members of Congress from both Democratic and Republican parties have bounced this idea around, but neither of them is willing to act on the idea when their party is in the White House. It's always a great idea when someone else is "controlling" spending. It's time for the American people to FORCE our government to live within a budget, regardless of which party is in the majority or in the White House. Of course, there will be times when it will be necessary to ignore the budget due to a national crisis. One of the ways to plan for these events is to include a "crisis" fund within the federal budget that could grow over the years when no crisis hits. If there's not enough in this fund, then Congress will have to "bite the bullet" and pass a new, temporary tax, tariff, or other fee to pay back the money borrowed to meet the crisis. Of course, states and individuals should be doing the same, using insurance and savings as best that they can to be ready for whatever crisis hits their area. I believe that a balanced budget amendment is the only way for American voters to force Congress to live within its means, just like you and I must do.

Amendment 28: Balanced Budget

Section 1. The President of the United States shall, on or before March 1st of each year, present to the House of Representatives a budget for the next fiscal year, which shall begin four months later, July 1st , and be effective until June 30th of the next year. Any disagreements over budgetary items defers to the President's submitted budget unless changed by a 60-40 vote of the members of the House. The Senate will no longer have input or vote in the budget process with the adoption of this amendment, and, therefore, does not vote on the budget adoption as its approval is not required. Section

Section 2. Congress shall create a National Disaster/Emergency Trust Fund whose sole purpose is to provide assistance to individuals, municipal/county/state governments, and federal facilities (such as military bases) when the President formally declares that such a disaster/emergency exists. The national budget shall include an annual deposit to said Trust Fund no less than 1.0% of total expected revenues. Annual deposits shall continue until said Trust Fund reaches "two trillion" dollars. This fund is reserved for any national disaster or emergency as approved by a 2/3rds vote of both houses of Congress. To be eligible for this assistance, individuals must already be carrying reasonable insurance to cover normal losses that could be expected from natural disasters as their personal finances allow (guidelines to be set by Congress). Municipal/county/state governments are required to set up and fund disaster/emergency trust funds of a similar nature to be eligible as well.

Section 3. Any deficit resulting from a budget shortfall in revenues or over-expenditure shall be automatically deducted from the previous year's budget figure amount set aside for National Defense; that figure will become the new budget figure for the next year's balanced budget. The primary fiduciary responsibility of the President and Congress is to spend no more than it raises through taxes, tariffs, etc.

Section 4. Congress is not restrained by an annual budget if it wishes to add new spending for what it considers important projects or programs. However, Congress must raise additional revenue (through additional taxes, not by scavenging funds from other budget items) to pay for the new spending which was not in the original budget. Said expenses and revenues must be approved by a 2/3rd vote of the House of Representatives and the Senate. The President's approval is not required due to the 2/3rds majority votes of both Houses of Congress.

Proposed Federal Budget Model Receipts:

Individual Income Tax Revenue $1,650,000,000,000
Corporate Income Tax Revenue 300,000,000,000***
Excise Taxes 100,000,000,000
Customs 36,000,000,000
Other: (Fines, seizures, penalties, etc.) 125,000,000,000

 Total Revenues $2,211,000,000,000

Disbursements:

Interest Payments on National Debt
$210,000,000,000**
Annual Retirement of Required National Debt Bonds
$350,000,000,000
Transfer to National Disaster Trust Fund
$50,000,000,000****
Congressional Branch Expenses $3,000,000,000
Supreme Court Branch Expenses $90,000,000,000
Defense Department $600,000,000,000
Justice Department $30,000,000,000
State Department $50,000,000,000

Treasure Department $15,000,000,000
Interior Department $190,000,000,000
Commerce Department $93,000,000,000
Citizen Services Department $280,000,000,000
Homeland Security Department $50,000,000,000
Central Intelligence Agency Department
$50,000,000,000

Total Disbursements $1,971,090,000,000
Surplus/(Deficit) $239,910,000,000*****

**The new bonds which will replace the older debt held by foreigners will carry a TAX EXEMPT 3% interest rate, paid annually. The national debt owed to social security or other governmental units will be temporarily "ignored," with no interest being accrued until foreign creditors are paid. It is pointless to pay interest to ourselves at this time. However, the $13 Billion which is owed back to taxpayers will be repaid in the future. If we lift the cap on social security contributions, the excess could be used to repay that portion of the debt once the new National Health system has stabilized. Once the foreign debt is gone, we can use the "freed funds" to fund the many public projects which are needed, to repay the former national debt, or to meet some other need that may exist in the future.

Debt will be repaid at $350 Billion a year for 20 years (approximately).

***Using this budget, corporate tax rates would be set at 30%, with the understanding that any reduction in taxes must be met with increased jobs, NOT increased dividends or salary increases for executives at those companies.

****The first four years of this balanced budget system will have $50 Billion deposited. After that, the amount will revert to the 1% of total income required by the new law.

*****Imagine what could be done with a budget surplus!! This is while paying off national debt, maintaining a fair tax rate for both individuals and corporations, and establishing a National Disaster Fund. Using this budget and the other changes which I propose, Social Security flourishes, those payment checks are increased to livable levels, a National Health Insurance Trust Fund is established, AND we begin to rebuild the country's infrastructure! By requiring our government (those servants of the people who we elect) to stick to a budget, pay off the shameful National Disgrace (debt), and setting aside funding for future disasters, **we, the people**, will put this country on the road to fiscal responsibility, something which we've not had for decades. Will it be easy? Not for a few years as the country pays off debt and learns to "live within its means." However, paraphrasing the immortal words of President John F. Kennedy, "We choose to require a balanced budget and pay off the national debt, not because they are easy, but because they are hard; because these goals will serve to organize and measure the best of our energies and skills, because that challenge is one that we are willing to accept..."

A Critical Issue:

"Health Care for citizens from birth to death" as ordered by YOUR doctor of choice should be instituted immediately! No co-pays, no deductibles, no lifetime limits! This is what Americans want, deserve, and will pay for themselves, no government interference or taxpayer funding!" While there are a number of critical issues for Americans today, my personal experience makes health care extremely important to me.

I would most likely not be alive today if it weren't for the Affordable Care Act. It was only because of that program that I could afford to go to a doctor, who, after learning of my family history, suggested that I visit the "cath lab." I came away with two stents and not long afterward a pacemaker for a condition called "bradycardia." I am extremely grateful for the Congress which passed the current health insurance program. Did it work the same for everyone? No, it did not and must be changed.

One program which has been proposed is "Medicare For All." As I understand it, it is an improvement. I could support that, but I believe that I have a better proposal. I propose that we move health insurance (and social security/medicare/medicaid) out of the hands of Congress and out of the national budget. I'm not a socialist; what I propose is NOT socialism. Government should not and would not be in charge of these, nor would the government fund them. **Citizens already pay for social security and medicare/medicaid through withholding taxes. We**

are entitled to them because we pay for them. Every time that I hear a politician complain that "entitlements are breaking the budget," I get angry! They don't belong in the budget!

Congress has never set withholding rates high enough to support the programs. My proposal does just that, along with extending health insurance withholding to "all forms of income except social security/private retirement payments."

First, and most important, under my program, "whatever your doctor (including dentists, chiropractors, and eye doctors) orders, it is covered, PERIOD!" There will be exceptions for nonessential surgeries such as cosmetic items. However, if these "cosmetic" procedures are critical to a patient's health, then they will be covered.

Second, "all prescription medications will be covered, PERIOD!" Because this is a national program, "drug/testing materials/devices will be negotiated on a national basis." This will drastically reduce the cost to this system. Some "drugs" will not be paid for just as most cosmetic surgeries will not be covered. Unless the drugs are determined to be "critical" to a patient, they will be optional, not paid for by the system. Not only will drugs, but ALL supplies will be negotiated on a "national" basis: needles, IV bags, sheets, everything will be negotiated as one national contract. That will insure that the American people get the lowest prices possible and won't be competing against other American hospitals and doctors.

Third, the system will be four-tiered. **The First Tier** is patients who will choose whatever doctor (if that doctor can handle additional patients) and insurance carrier that they prefer. Doctors will be paid a fixed amount monthly by insurance carriers for patients for whom they provide care. That fee will be set nationally based on local, regional, and national costs. Doctors can be switched at anytime; if you don't like your doctor, find another one. Once a year, people will be able to switch insurance carriers if you are not happy with their services.

The second tier is insurance companies. They are free to advertise and provide extra services; however, insurance companies will be paid the same amount each month for each person, regardless of age, gender, health issues, etc. for basic services. Insurance companies will not be allowed to refuse coverage to anyone who applies who is an American citizen, regardless of past medical history. Those questions will not appear on the application (only name, address, and previous insurance carrier so that the previous carrier can be notified of the change and will discontinue paying for services after that date.). Insurance carriers will be paid a monthly fee set by the system, adjusted for regional and local costs. Obviously, the cost of living in San Francisco is not the same as in Watson, Louisiana. Insurance companies will increase profits by increasing the number of patients which they have. Extra costs such as surgeries, cancer treatments, etc. will be reimbursed to the insurance carriers by the national health system itself. Insurance carriers will be responsible for auditing and monitoring doctors to discourage waste and to prevent abuses.

The third tier is pharmacies and medical equipment and other suppliers. They will be paid based on negotiated contracts. All patients have to do is walk in and provide their medical ID along with proof that they are who they say they are (to prevent fraud), sign, and maintain the receipt for when an auditor appears to verify that they actually ordered/received" said drugs/equipment/supplies.

Finally, the **fourth tier** is the Citizen's National Health Insurance Trust Fund. The system will maintain a national office and regional and state offices where contracts will be negotiated as needed, payments to insurance carriers will be made, auditing will be handled, complaints will be handled from patients, insurance carriers, and contractors, and collected funds will be protected and invested as necessary. The simplest way to explain the system is that patients will have no out of pocket costs for covered visits/drugs/surgeries/etc. Insurance companies will pay doctors monthly and reimburse doctors, hospitals, and certain contractors for extra services. The National system will reimburse insurance companies for extra expenses related to surgery, therapies, equipment, etc. Prescribed drugs and equipment that patients receive outside of a doctor's office or hospital will be paid by the national system. Drug prices, hospital prices, equipment and other services, etc. will be negotiated between the system and those entities.

What are the benefits of this program?

1. Citizens are covered from birth to death for whatever they need at no cost to them, PERIOD! There are no co-pays, no premiums, no out-of-pocket costs. Whatever the citizen earns is subject to withholding at a fixed percentage that is set by law and can change only once a year to adjust for

inflation/new technology costs/etc. I believe that 15% will be sufficient once the system is in place for several years.

2. Employers (and the self employed) will no longer have to provide health insurance for their employees. Non citizen employees will have the same deductions for health, but those payments will be provided to the employee for his/her private health insurance coverage. (There will still be a need for workman's compensation coverage, though it should be MUCH LOWER since most claims will be handled by the health system itself.

3. Insurance companies will only be allowed to have a 10% after-tax profit. However, there will be incentive programs down the road which will allow the "best" companies to profit from reducing waste, encouraging healthy programs, etc. The monthly payments to insurance companies and doctors will be adjusted on an annual basis, changing based on many factors, some of which are patients comments, cost controls, complaints, late-payments, etc.

How do we pay for this system? This national health program will be expensive, but we already pay for it now! Premiums, co-pays, deductibles, personal bankruptcies, mortgages, fund-raisers, donations, and any other imaginable way to raise money are used now. Of course, many people simply go without seeing a doctor until they end up in the emergency room and cost hospitals and taxpayers who are forced to cover illnesses which could have either been prevented or mitigated with early intervention. Can Americans really afford this system? How can we not? At present those citizens who have the funds just write checks for premiums, co-pays, deductibles, and those medical procedures that insurance doesn't pay for now. Those citizens who don't have the funds do one of several things: avoid medical treatments, do without something important like food or prescriptions, or file bankruptcy when the bills just pile up to the point where they can't be ignored. Finally, there are the millions of citizens who just don't go to the doctor unless it's the emergency room after being delivered by an ambulance. Meanwhile, the insurance companies and pharmaceutical manufacturers rake in the profits with little concern for citizens.

The citizens of the United States have long deserved full medical care for what they need, when they need it! The dollars exist; don't let anyone tell you that we can't afford what most other "civilized/ modern" countries already have. The difference is that we won't be depending on our government to fund it. No one wants the government in his/her business. I certainly don't! So, why do I say that we can afford the increase in withholding taxes, along with the several other innovative taxes that I will propose? Let's look at where Americans now spend their "disposable (or not)" incomes.

1. Gross gaming revenues: $160 Billion (includes lottery, casinos, etc.)

2. Sporting event revenues: $72 Billion (all sources)

3. Movies, music, cable industry revenues: $170 Billion

4. Restaurant revenues: $800 Billion

5. Hospitality Industry revenues: $210 Billion

6. Airline Revenues: $750 Billion

7. Automobile Industry revenues: $1.4 Trillion

These alone total $3.56 Trillion dollars, most of which is considered "discretionary" spending. Almost none of these are required such as rent, food, clothing, utilities. Granted some of them are required for a variety of personal reasons, but the vast majority are things which a person/family could live without and still meet those budget items which can't be ignored to survive. This is more than all the medical expenses nationwide in 2015.

We CAN afford this program! I propose that ALL income be subject to both social security and health insurance contributions. Only the un-taxed portion of income will be newly taxed. For those people without investment income, rents, etc., there will be no additional contribution. By doing this, billions of dollars will now be subject to contributions to the social security and health care systems. In addition, the funds collected will not go through the Federal Budget; they will only be funneled through the IRS to the CNHITFC. Rates will change periodically as costs rise and fall. Okay, what about "non-American citizens," visitors, temporary workers, students, etc. who are here but not American citizens? ALL of those people will be required to purchase "temporary" visitors insurance (employers will not differentiate between citizens/non-citizens when paying wages, insurance/social security contributions, or other benefits) (non-citizen employees will have the employer portion of insurance used to reduce their policy premiums, but the social security portion does not accrue to them unless they are citizens), a category that will certainly grow from this system through independent insurance companies who see an opportunity. The cost and coverage and collection of these insurance premiums will be up to the insurance companies, though the government will provide guidelines to prevent "gouging" or "profiteering."

Naturally, should someone appear at an emergency room with a life-threatening injury or illness, he/she will be treated. These people will also be required to provide insurance or pay for the services, or, at the discretion of the hospital, be forgiven as some hospitals do now. Realistically, the 15% figure (15% personal/15% employer) that I am using might not be enough to cover all medical (health, vision, and dental) expenses during the first few years. It is more likely, in the short term, that excess social security contributions will need to be used while the system stabilizes as people freely begin to seek medical attention which has been ignored in the past. However, the difference might be made up by adding a few new "taxes;" those would provide the extra funding needed.

I propose a new 3% tax on ALL financial instrument transactions, transfers, stock sales, commodity sales, bond trading, mortgage instruments, etc. This, according to my "rough" estimates, would provide more than enough added funding to create a system whereby ALL Americans would be covered. I also propose the following be adopted to help reduce the cost of this system to citizens. These consumer products are targeted (others might be suggested as well) because their consumption has a direct effect on health, thus medical costs. These taxes would go through local systems and funneled into the CNHITFC. I'm sure that the Office of Management and Budget (OMB) could provide excellent rates and dollars raised, something which I can't do with only access to the internet information that is available.

A National Sales Tax targeted for Health Insurance support:

1. Tobacco (Cost to health industry by tobacco products=$170 billion a year)

2. All soft drink beverages

3. All candies, confections, desserts, candy bars, cakes, cookies, etc., and frozen dessert items (ice cream, frozen yogurt, etc.)

4. All crackers, chips, and other packaged snacks

5. Alcohol/marijuana products

A simple way to implement these types of taxes, for the most part, would be to place this tax at the source, on sales between producers of ingredients and food producers. That way, each product doesn't have to be taxed at the retail level, which would cost consumers more. However, I am open to the best method of imposing such a tax. While this proposed system is not perfect and will need considerable work by doctors, insurance companies, Congress, and the public to be implemented and monitored so that it becomes a cost-effective system, it does combine two ideas: comprehensive insurance for everyone and as little government involvement as possible. I don't believe that it's possible to have one without the other.

This is NOT a government-run program. It will be managed by doctors, insurance companies, and citizens ONLY, with the legislative and legal assistance of Congress. Will there be issues and problems to be resolved? Of course, but that's the case now with the confusing conglomeration of companies and policies and coverages that we have now! The differences are two. This program will provide health coverage for EVERYONE, not just those who can afford whatever they need, AND is will provide transparency as to costs and profits of the providers. American citizens will be covered from birth to death with this program. If we don't like something, we can negotiate a fix. Can you do that now with your insurance company?

"**Watchdogs**" will be encouraged to independently monitor the new system for our protection (citizens). Contributions are based on total income; the following computations would apply. **How the money will be spent:** There are approximately 300 million American Citizens, those for whom this program is created (a similar plan will be created for non-citizens later). By my best research estimates, the average cost of current insurance policies that have no co-pays or deductibles is $210 per person per month (total premiums divided by 300 million people) plus $20 for dental and $20 for vision coverages. My projection is that insurance companies will be given $250 per person covered per month, which equals $900 Billion per year. For this, insurance companies will provide all preventive care, normal visits as needed, and all medications/procedures prescribed by doctors. For those items which fall under a list which will be developed, though it will cover those expensive treatments such as surgery, cancer treatments, drug addiction treatment, certain mental health treatments, oral surgeries, crowns, etc. For those items, the insurance companies will apply for reimbursement from the Clearinghouse, which will do so for a pre-determined amount, but citizens will NOT have co-pays, deductibles, or any other "created" out-of-pocket expense. Again, all drugs and medical equipment prices will be determined through a national negotiation process. Any company that wishes to sell to the American market will have to negotiate a national or regional price. We WILL get the best cost savings this way. This is the only way to keep costs down and provide all American Citizens with the best medical care at the best price in the world. We have paid too much for too long. With this program, we will lead the world, not pay the highest prices! Citizens AND employers will no longer be concerned with medical insurance coverages or payments. All employers will be on equal footing with every other employer just as every citizen will be able to move from job to job without worrying about health insurance/medical needs!

Who will control this program? There will be a board of governors, all bonded and sworn by law, chosen in a variety of ways but with one object, to provide the most cost-effective, non-partisan, color-blind, gender-blind, disease-blind program which will serve ALL CITIZENS EQUALLY. There will be no special treatment or special favors granted by a "governor." This group will be responsible for oversight, selection of management (who will receive salaries as though public servants not private enterprise companies), negotiating contracts with all parties (in coordination with management), and enforcing rules, procedures, and penalties for violations of said. The governors will consist of 50% male, 50 % female, overall, who will be voting members. Two members will be appointed (one male, one female) from each of the following groups: AARP (American Association of Retired Persons) Department of Veteran's Affairs A.M.A. (American Medical Association) The Pharmaceutical Industry (unsure how to do that) National Hospital Association Six nationally-recognized Citizen health advocates, three men and three women. (exactly how they will be selected is not determined at this point, but they must not be political appointees) Non-voting members who will be appointed as liaison to Congress and the President (it is preferred that both genders will be represented): Members of House of Representatives-one Democrat, one Republican, one Independent (if possible) Members of the Senate-one Republican, one Democrat, one Independent (if possible) Official from the White House as assigned by the President. The governors will be appointed for two-year terms and may be re-appointed once. If members choose to leave, they will be replaced by someone of the same gender as soon as practical for their own two-year term.

This will not be a secret organization; transparency will be mandatory. The media will have complete access to meetings but only as observers. All contracts and decisions will be made public, but there will not be a "public comment" period. Governors will receive a reasonable "stipend" for their time and expenses, but those stipends will be publicly disclosed on a monthly basis. Any "abuse" of funds, allowances, expenses will be grounds for dismissal from the Board by majority vote of its members. Members will select a "non-industry" "Foreman" to lead meetings and discussions. (Only Civilians, Members of A.A.R.P., or the Dept. of Veteran's Affairs are eligible to be "Foreman." While there are other details and decisions to be made, this is how I see this organization being supervised. The day-to-day work will be done by the hired executives, staff, and support personnel. Salaries, benefits, etc. will be established by the Board of Governors with the assistance of the Executive Manager, hired and supervised by the Board.

The Citizen's National Health Insurance Trust Fund will be organized like any major business but will exist as a "co-op" for the benefit of all American citizens. It must be independent of political influence. After all, the funds and expenses are for us. We will finally no longer have to worry about medical care that we need. Health should improve when all citizens can visit a dentist or optometrist or any other doctor that is needed. Hopefully, the goal of doctors will be able to move away from "fixing preventable problems" to preventing expensive treatments. This won't be a perfect system, but if people begin to change their lifestyles so that they stay healthier longer and follow their doctor's advice, the cost to all of us will go down, the withholdings will fall, and the standard of health in the United States will once again "lead the world."

That's what Americans deserve and can have once we take politics out of health care! Three Medical Issues of Note Generally, government has no place in medical decisions. Politics should also remain separate from an individual's right to make treatment decisions. What right do I have to tell another person that one decision is right or wrong? Two specific instances illustrate my position on "life" choices. First, physician-assisted suicide: No one, especially government officials, should have the right to prevent any adult from ending his/her life. While other people may disagree with the choice, if any person files a legal document relieving a physician of any legal responsibility two weeks prior to said death, that should be possible. The two week notice would give people of interest, including the physician, a period of comment and to say their "goodbyes." Arrangements for the disposal of the remains are required before a physician may assist with the termination of life. Second, termination of pregnancy: No one, especially government officials, should have the right to force a woman to carry a pregnancy past 20 weeks. The use of "religious beliefs" to prevent the termination is a violation of the U.S. Constitution's separation of "church and state." The 20-week timetable was a compromise between those who oppose any termination and those who oppose any limit. (Roe v. Wade) Terminations after 20 weeks would only be allowed for the safety of the mother or in the case of known birth defects which the mother (hopefully along with the agreement by the father- however that isn't necessary since it is the woman's body) believes would be unacceptable.

A better priority should be to PREVENT UNWANTED PREGNANCY! Free access to birth control, all working methods, including the "morning after pill" which prevents pregnancy. If people truly want to prevent pregnancies, then the key is education supported by birth control methods, which includes a realistic understanding that simply teaching "abstention" isn't enough.

While I firmly believe that the government (all levels) should stay out of medical treatment decisions, the one area where I must disagree with that policy is the emergency treatment of minors. Physicians must be allowed to provide life-saving decisions, even over the objection of parents/guardians. In addition, immunization decisions are the prerogative of parents until those children either attend public schools or become a hazard to the public in general. While I understand the hesitation/concerns of many parents concerning vaccines, the safety of the public has to come first. This does not prevent a parent from taking legal action to fight that immunization. Parents still reserve the right to sue for any negative impact on their child if given, resulting in injury or death of the child. While a negative result is highly unlikely, it does happen.

Social Security-A Better Future

We are often told that Social Security, Medicare, and Medicaid are "bankrupting" the country. Perhaps that is true in the way that the system is working at present. It's an easy fix! I propose several things which will not only prevent that and stabilize these systems but make it possible for our seniors to receive larger payments. Currently, the entitlement programs (so designated because we pay for them; they aren't social welfare!) appear as part of the national budget. THEY SHOULD NOT! Both Social Security and Medicare should NOT be a part of the federal budget; they should operate independently with Congress auditing and supervising only.

They won't cost the taxpayers a dime because they are NOT funded by tax dollars; they are and will continue to be funded like any retirement system, through citizen contributions. Those who don't pay into the system will not benefit from it! (Obviously, certain citizens who are designated as unable to contribute because of either physical or mental disabilities from birth or later in life, according to guidelines established by Congress, will be exempted from this rule.)

First, I propose that we lift the cap on contributions. In 2017, social security/Medicare deductions stopped at $127,200. In the future, CEO's, wealthy investors, famous athletes and entertainment celebrities, and others making millions of dollars a year will contribute much more to Social Security and

Citizen's National Health Insurance Trust Funds. People are still free to contribute to private retirement systems/ health insurance systems (if they so choose), though there will no longer be a deduction against their taxable income for private programs. Social Security Contributions to the Trust Fund WITH CAP are $232,662,261,000 (6.2%)

Total Contributions Without Cap are $505,583,758,000 (5%)

Difference is $272,921,497,000. How long would it take for social security trust fund to be safe and solvent if the Cap is removed? What would it hurt the wealthy?

Keep in mind that these figures don't include the employers' contributions that match the withholding figures. (This information comes from the 2014 IRS figures available on the internet.) In addition, when extending social security payments to "all income" sources, the contributions grow even higher, allowing for citizens to receive higher payments, something which can only contribute to more sales and more jobs in the economy. The excess, as determined by a fiduciary, could decide how much of this could be contributed to the CNHITFC as needed to cover medical needs. Isn't it time for Congress to lift the caps, not to mention extending contributions to all income?

B. Second, I propose increasing payments to recipients. The payments have always been limited by other income so that the "wealthy" don't draw from a system which was intended to support those in need during their elder years. I propose that payments start at age 60 and are not reduced by other income until the combined total of social security and other income (regardless of its source) reaches $50,000, my base, non-taxable income level. We have a moral responsibility to better care for seniors than we do at present; increasing social security payments can be a start toward that goal. Anyone who calls "social security" socialism doesn't understand what socialism is. It is, according to www.merriam-webster.com dictionary, as follows: **"Socialism is –** any of various economic and political theories advocating collective or governmental ownership and administration of the MEANS of production and distribution of goods." How does this apply to the social security "retirement" system or an independent, nongovernmental National Health Insurance Trust Fund? Our Social Security system was created to be a dependable retirement system for all American citizens meeting certain criteria including working a specific period of time to "pay into the system." Funding was fine for a number of years, but the program was not built for society with an economic system that would grow dramatically along with the cost of living. Only by truly funding this necessary "safeguard" which most older Americans now depend on to survive can we assure that those who work hard for a lifetime will not be without a "life preserver." Doing this does not prevent people from having other savings programs or investments. It only enhances them. However, in today's world, most people are doing well to just pay the bills, raise their families, educate the children, and maintain their health; for too many private retirement systems are only a dream. By extending payments to ALL INCOME SOURCES and ALL INCOME, NOT JUST A LIMITED LEVEL, social security can become a true retirement system. Those who need it will have it; those who don't will have helped fellow Americans enjoy their "golden years" rather than struggle through depending on "soup kitchens" and "food banks" to survive. The additional contributions that people will make will hurt no one.

Tax Reform For EVERYONE!
(not just the wealthy)

A Simplified Individual Tax Return: I am proposing a new income tax system, not just a tax cut for the short term. The point of this proposal is to LEVEL THE TAX FIELD FOR ALL AMERICANS! The basis for this return is that there will be no more deductions for anything! In addition, "special" tax rates and exemptions will be abolished. "Capital gains" and the "oil depletion allowance" will no longer exist. This system takes the position that all people should pay the same tax rate, regardless of personal lifestyle decisions, income sources, or personal expenses.

In addition, **taxes are filed as individuals**, not according to marital status. "Children" will have tax returns filed for them by guardians if income exists, regardless of the amount. What people choose to do with their after-tax income is their business, not government's. I suggest that each person test this system and see how much difference there is in their taxes compared to the previous system. It is simpler, fairer, and does not place an undue burden on anyone. This new tax return reflects the changes in social security and National Health Insurance that I am also proposing.

In addition to the new tax return, I am also proposing several other changes to the tax system at. this point:

47

A. Sales taxes must be imposed on all "internet" sales. State and local sales tax collections are being hurt by these tax-free sales.

B. Abolishment of the "gift tax" when coming from previously taxed resources. Gifts of land, stocks, or anything else of "value" will have a transfer value that existed for the donor so that only the gain to the recipient will be taxed when sold in the future. Gift taxes only hinder people from sharing their good fortune with others. With the elimination of donations as a tax deduction, it only makes sense to do away with taxes on gifts. While the wealthy might benefit greatly, it also allows "average" citizens to share their good fortune with others, whether the recipients are related or not. States still retain the right to impose taxes as they see fit. (Lottery winnings are already heavily taxed, so if a winner chooses to share his/her already taxed winnings, there will be no federal tax on that gift. States reserve the right to tax according to their own laws.)

C. Abolishment of the federal "gasoline tax." A gallon of gasoline has about 19 cents of federal excise tax. Diesel has about 25 cents per gallon. At the same time that I propose dropping this tax, I also propose that all highways be the responsibility of each state, whether interstate or not. States are better equipped to maintain their roads and should be the ones using fuel taxes to pay for those improvements. Should there be a need for new interstate highways, the concerned states would need to negotiate help from Congress to build them. Most states don't need new interstate highways; they need more improvements on their own roads.

D. A new 10% (ten percent) "sales tax" on "luxury items," items sold at auction, and real estate valued at $500,000 or more will be imposed to supplement federal income taxes. "Luxury items" are those such as second homes, yachts, private/corporate airplanes, automobiles over $50,000, liquor/wine/beer sold for more than $50 per standard bottle, entertainment/sporting event tickets over $50, and other items which will be established by Congress.

E. A new 10% (ten percent) "hotel/motel" room tax will be imposed on a nightly basis. During a disaster, this tax will be suspended as directed by FEMA for those rooms housing disaster victims.

*****In addition, ALL TAXES collected by employers and businesses and individuals will be legally required to be deposited daily into "tax dedicated checking accounts." These funds do not belong to those collecting them; they belong to the government and will be audited on a regular basis to make certain that no business or entity gets into trouble because they can't pay their sales or employment taxes at the end of the month. Once a month the bank accounts will automatically be forwarded to the collecting agency, along with a report showing the sales or employment taxes collected or required by the businesses. Failure to fully comply with the deposits or transfers will result in criminal penalties.

I estimate that using this flat rate, with no deductions, would generate more than $1.65 Trillion of income taxes from individuals (per the chart below though increased to allow for increases since 2014). Every taxpayer would be treated the same; 25% of their income in excess of $50,000 would be the rate.

Whether rich or poor, the tax rate would be the same. The total tax collected will actually be higher than previously because "special interest" tax deductions now on the books will be removed with the institution of my tax plan. Exactly how much more will be generated cannot be determined at this point. The IRS or the Congressional Budget Office would be better able to make that determination.

Corporate rates would be set at 30%, a fair and competitive rate. Over the years, the tax system has become a bloated list of special deductions, tax exemptions, and various rates designed by those who had the most to benefit, adding a few for the average citizen to claim, a pretense that this was designed for all Americans, when, in fact, most of the changes over the years really just benefit the wealthy or investors or businesses to produce more profits. If those profits had been shared with the employees, it would have made sense. However, that has rarely been the case. A good case in point is the latest "tax cut" which was given to businesses. Yes, a few small companies did pass along some of the "windfall" in the form of bonuses. What I read, however, is that most did not; many used this "windfall" to buy back stocks, thereby increasing the value of the remaining stock to major stockholders and executives. What I am proposing to do is simple, would tax very little legislation, and, politically speaking, a bonanza since approximately 75 million Americans will not pay any income taxes. True, their withholdings will increase for social security/national health protection, but they also won't be paying health insurance premiums any longer. I think that might translate to lots of voters supporting the party which passes this program!

National Defense Policy

Regardless of what any "politician" may say, the United States has been and always will be the only true "Superpower" on Earth in this modern age. There are several pretenders, but they do not have the resources, the "manpower (including women)," the training, or the firepower of the U.S. That must not and will not ever change. We should start acting like the leader of the free world. How? The following policies should be implemented immediately:

1. All U.S. allies are immediately under the "nuclear/conventional weapon" protection umbrella in case of threat or attack by a non-ally. That doesn't mean that our allies aren't required to maintain their own defense forces. We expect to be their partner, not a mercenary force for their protection.

2. Any attempt by a foreign nation or a radical group to interfere, endanger, or harm any American citizen will be met with whatever response is deemed appropriate, including the use of armed forces, economic or diplomatic sanctions, or cyber actions will be used with or without the assistance of our allies.

3. The United States will continue to do research into new weapons systems, for deployment as required on land, under the sea, in the air, and in space. Defense spending not only protects us, but it also helps maintain technological advantage for the United States and provides thousands of jobs for Americans. Under my leadership, this will continue and be

supplemented by stricter auditing to prevent fraud and waste.

4. At present I know of no reason why there should be any change in the Triad system which currently exists, but the United States reserves the right to extend that to a space-based system as well.

5. Veterans should also be able to visit local physicians for whatever services are needed, at their discretion. As citizens, veterans will receive the same "doctor ordered" services that any other citizen receives. Special services that might only be available through the V.A. would be reserved for Vets.

6. We must conduct a thorough review of all "security" policies and "secrets" with regard to UFO's, Area 51, Wright Patterson AFB, and all other Top Secret material with a promise to release any and all materials that a committee of appointed citizens deem "safe" to share with American citizens. In addition, the documentation still unreleased from the JFK assassination investigation should be released immediately. These "secrets" should no longer be "secrets." The American people have a right to know and have been kept in the dark for too many years.

The defense of the United States and its allies is the number one priority of the government of the United States. All other issues will and must take a backseat to National Defense!

National Public Service

It is time to bring Congress back down to Earth! For too long, members of both the House of Representatives and the Senate have seen themselves as "elite." **They are "public servants," "employees"** as it were of "We, the People." They vote themselves pay raises and benefits and special retirement. Who do they think that they are, ROYALTY? It is time for voters to "knock them down a notch" so that they might remember who is their boss! **In reality, they are "state" employees of the voters of the states from which they were elected**. They should be treated the same way. There also need to be limits on the years which they can serve to prevent "old habits" from stagnating future progress. I propose two changes which will bring them back down to reality, the reality that they work for us, not special interest groups and the wealthy!

First: Term Limits for ALL elected or appointed public officials: One of the problems which we have always faced is having people sit in jobs for 30 or 40 years in Congress and other government jobs. The lifeblood of our country is youth! We need an amendment to do just that. My own thoughts are as follows: President (and Vice-President), one six-year term; members of the Senate, two six-year terms; House of Representatives, three three-year terms (1/3 elected each year); Supreme Court members, one ten-year term (one being appointed each year by the President with the consent of a majority of the Senate); all other federal judges, one ten-year term; and all appointed federal employees are limited to ten years (total service) in various positions. These limits would not prevent a person from being a member of the House, then the Senate, and then as President. I'm flexible with these limits, but I believe that there is much talent being wasted in our young people. Someone with great gifts or special skills could still be utilized in government service by other means, such as actual "employee" positions or being appointed to an administrative or Cabinet position. If "the future belongs to the young," then we must put more of our future in the hands of the "young!"

Second, I propose **Amendment 30: Term Limits**

Section 1. The President of the United States will be restricted to one, six-year term, a maximum of eight years if succeeding to the Presidency from the Vice-Presidency. The eight years are not required to be continuous service.

Section 2. The Vice-President may not serve more than six years in said office.

Section 3. Persons may serve no more than two six-year terms as Senator. If appointed to fill an empty seat, a person may serve no more than a total of fourteen years as a Senator.

Section 4. Persons may serve no more than three three-year terms as a member of the House of Representatives. If appointed to fill an empty seat, a person may serve no more than eleven years as a member of the House of Representatives.

Section 5. Supreme Court Justices may serve no more than ten years. Every year the President, on June 1st, will nominate three candidates to be the next Supreme Court Justice. Said candidates will have been investigated by the F.B.I. following a designated protocol established by the Senate. The Senate will have until July 1st to call for public comments before conducting public job interviews over a three-week period before voting on said candidate. If the Senate does not approve one of the candidates (simple majority vote is required), the President may then select the candidate of his/her choice who will take the place of the most senior member then sitting on the Court on October 1st. The most senior member will be the Justice who has served the longest on the Supreme Court. Should a Justice leave or be removed from the Court, that seat will remain vacant until such time as it would have normally fallen into the replacement rotation. Until all of the current Justices have been replaced, one each year, the ten year limit will not apply to them. With the adoption of this amendment, their terms are no longer for life.

Section 6. No person shall serve in any non-elected position with the federal government (Supreme Court Justices are considered elected for this section) for more than ten years. That does not preclude anyone from leaving an appointed position and being "hired" into a civil service position; such employment would then be subject to standard civil service rules concerning longevity.

Section 7: Any elected or appointed official (whether state, local, or federal) who wishes to seek an elected office must resign his/her current position before filing to run for said office. Failure to do so will automatically void the filing.

Third: Congressional members will be "State" employees: Rather than having members of Congress paid out of the U.S. Treasury, I propose that each state set salaries, staff sizes and salaries, and expenses for each member, along with paying them out of the state budget. They are, after all, state employees. They should be treated as such, participating in the same benefit programs that other state employees do, adjusted for their office requirements.

Fourth. I propose **Amendment 31: Congressional Status and Compensation**

Section 1. Members of the Senate and the House of Representatives will hereafter be designated State Employees; they will no longer be compensated out of the federal budget.

Section 2. States are responsible for the compensation of said members, including, but not limited to salary, living allowance, travel allowance, retirement arrangements, and disability coverage, just as each state does its other employees.

Section 3. Congressional staffs, including the appropriate size of said staff, will also be the responsibility of each state, including, but not limited to, salary, retirement arrangements, disability coverage, and any travel/accommodations deemed appropriate.

Section 4. Office space for all members of Congress will continue to be provided as in the past. By adopting these amendments, Congress will be more responsive to its voters, less likely to become "stagnant" political stooges of a party, and more responsive to voters needs and concerns. Sure, there will always be some elected or appointed and are only there to serve themselves but by limiting their time in Washington, it will be easier to get rid of them.

Abolish the Electoral College and Return to a Paper Ballot

There is something terribly wrong when the candidate for President of the United States is chosen by a select group of "political pawns" instead of American voters. How did we get this system? "The Constitutional Convention of 1787 considered several methods of electing the President, including selection by Congress, by the governors of the states, by the state legislatures, by a special group of Members of Congress chosen by lot, and by direct popular election. Late in the convention, the matter was referred to the Committee of Eleven on Postponed Matters, which devised the electoral college system in its original form. This plan, which met with widespread approval by the delegates, was incorporated into the final document with only minor changes. It sought to reconcile differing state and federal interests, provide a degree of popular participation in the election, give the less populous states some additional leverage in the process by providing "senatorial" electors, preserve the presidency as independent of Congress, and generally insulate the election process from political manipulation."

I can understand why the delegates devised this system and sought to balance the needs and concerns of citizens of both the large and the small states. The country was young and growing; there were worries about influence from more developed/

prosperous parts of the country. However, those concerns have little value. My own opinion is that the electoral college was a useful tool during our early history, a period when there was little formal education and even less media coverage of issues and news. That is no longer the case. People no longer need to choose someone to vote in their place. Several of the past few elections have demonstrated that when there is a popular vote for one candidate and an electoral vote for a different candidate, the nation suffers, is torn, angry that the will of a majority of the voters doesn't matter. That is terribly wrong! An election should bring out the "will" of the majority of voters, not the political desires of a select group. **THAT IS NOT DEMOCRACY!** The electoral college is an obsolete system of selecting our President, one which can distort our political process. It's time has long since passed!

I propose the following amendment. **Popular Vote Amendment**

Section 1. Beginning with the first Presidential election held following the adoption of this amendment, the offices of President and Vice-President will be elected by popular vote. The electoral college system is hereby abolished. Whichever Presidential candidate receives the most popular votes is deemed the winner, along with his/her Vice-Presidential running mate.

I would also recommend that the United States, in all elections for national office (at least), return to using paper ballots and discontinuing the use of electronic machines. I believe that if it hasn't happened yet, it is only a matter of time before an election is changed by a person or organization through hacking voter machines. Will it take longer to count, yes, but it need only apply to Congress and the President/Vice-Presidential votes. That's not asking too much of both voters and poll workers. In addition, I believe that voting across the country should take place over a two week period (Monday-Saturday) beginning the first Monday in November at 8 a.m. and ending each day at 8 p.m. Votes would be counted by a committee representing each major party (each party must have received at least 10% of the vote in the previous national election)(selected by the party), certified at the end by these members, and observed/verified by an appropriate member of local law enforcement. The results would then be provided to the Secretary of State of each state, who would be responsible for certifying the results and then providing those tallies to both the Federal Election Commission and the authorized representatives of all news media who ask for them. However, no results would be allowed to be released until all votes are reported and final totals, possibly excluding absentee ballots, if they have not been opened and counted, though they should be on the final day of voting by the appropriate authorities (at the precincts or county, etc. level by, again representatives of each party should be doing the counting) are certified for state races.

Presidential /Vice-Presidential voting should not be reported to the public until ALL STATES HAVE CLOSED THEIR POLLS! Any national election (Congress or Presidential) which results in a winning margin of less than 1% must be automatically recounted the next day with those results reported in the same manner. Any candidate may ask for a recount if the margin of loss is less than 2% without being charged for the recount. Any candidate asking for a recount where the margin is greater than 2% must pay for said recount at an amount designated by the Federal Election Commission.

The purpose of using the paper ballot is to reassure Americans that their votes are being counted and that there is no fraud involved in the counting process. While it may make little difference and will likely cause the tabulation process to take longer and be more expensive, that is a small price to pay for public confidence in the election results.

Presidential Eligibility. To prevent another situation where a President could have financial or other potential investment/other conflicts of interest, new ironclad regulations must be established to prevent candidates from ascending to the White House and possibly using (whether directly or indirectly) that position to profit through policies of the administration. Whether this means a new constitutional amendment or simply laws with authority to prevent such a candidate to be designated qualified to be President or Vice-President. (Should anyone in the line of succession be called upon to fill the office of either President or Vice-President, that person would also have to meet these qualifications within 30 days of assuming the office of President.)

1. Candidates must be "natural" citizens, born of one or more American citizens, regardless of where the actual birth occurred.

2. Candidates must, after being elected to the office of President or Vice-President, either simply divest all financial interests or put said investments into a TRUE BLIND TRUST, one which is controlled by a fiduciary whose only contact with the candidates or associates will be to supply them with tax documents so that annual income taxes can be filed or upon leaving office, at which time all records must be turned over to the candidates.

3. Anyone who wishes to run for President must certify that he/she meets all criteria for sitting as President before appearing on any primary ballot, including the following:

A. Release the previous ten years tax returns.

B. Release a certified copy of his/her birth certificate.

C. Release a current physical/mental examination from a nationally recognized medical facility, one which has, in addition to current testing, had access to previous medical records.

D. Release the results of a detailed criminal background check.

E. Candidates for national office must not have participated in an attempted overthrow of the government or given aid and comfort to those who have. Any public support for such illegal actions by others disqualifies a person from holding national public office.

F. No person shall be eligible to run for President or Vice-President if he or she has reached or will have reached the age of 65 by election day.

4. Eligibility for national office is determined by federal statute, NOT state laws. Individual states may not refuse to allow any federally qualified candidate from appearing on its ballot.

Campaign Finance Reform
(Citizen's United)

Since I'm not a lawyer and have no business arguing the point of the corruption of many in our political process, I must rely on common sense. While I have read and generally understand the Supreme Court's reasoning and decision in the "Citizen's United" case, it is apparent to me that the law, possibly even the U.S. Constitution, needs to be amended to make it clear that only people are protected by our Constitution and Bill of Rights. Regardless on which side of this particular case you stand, it should concern you that any non-human entity (corporation, partnership, etc.), through the power of its resources (cash, influence, etc.), could change the outcome of any election at any level of government. If you are on the losing side of an important issue simply because a small group (small being a relative term) has immense wealth, power, or influence which cannot be matched, you'll learn the hard lesson that our system of government, which is supposed to be "fair and unbiased," can soon be "unfair and one-sided" in its decisions. Right now, money means power through its ability to hire lawyers, buy media coverage, and intimidate people. Common sense should tell us that, since only people vote, only people should be allowed the freedom of speech and the other protections of the U.S. Constitution.

We already have organizations which people can join or organize to support candidates for office. They are called "political parties," fair and efficient or not. PAC's (political action committees) are not political parties; they are "political lobbies" which, in many cases, only seek to serve the wealthy who wish to pursue policies which make them wealthier! Yes, anyone can set up a PAC, but it's the power of the money which a PAC can raise and wield that has the potential to change the outcome of an election.

In my opinion, corporations do not and should not be treated as people. Regardless, every American should be concerned about the power of financial influence in our government and society. There is a way to, if not prevent this abuse, at least mitigate the influence which money can have on our election process: make it transparent!

For this reason, I propose that the following be adopted, either as a **Constitutional amendment or simply federal law**. Below it is in the form of an amendment.

Amendment : Campaign Finance

Section 1: There are no restrictions on what an individual, using personal funds, may spend on his/her campaign for Federal, elected office (President, Vice-President, Senator, or member of the House of Representatives).

Section 2: Funds raised, donated, or otherwise contributed by others directly to a candidate's campaign are restricted. The limit on these non-personal funds is determined by the number of registered voters in a particular election, ire. number of registered voters (regardless of party affiliation) in a House of Representative District or total registered voters nationally in a Presidential election. Those totals will be determined by each state's office which is responsible for such data. The limit is $1 for each registered voter. If there are a million registered voters in a district (regardless of party affiliation), then that is the amount which may be spent by the candidate by any candidate. (This must not be construed to mean that a particular party candidate can only spend according to the number of registered voters from his/her party; it is the total registered voters that each candidate will use as the amount that can be spent by said candidate.)

Section 3: Donations, which are restricted to individuals (business entities may not contribute to political candidates or direct funds to individuals with the purpose of spending those funds for a political purpose), made directly to a candidate are limited to $100 per election (a primary is considered a separate election). Records of donations (name, address, phone number, and amount of donation) must be kept by each campaign and be available to the public or media, at any time, upon request (if printed, a reasonable charge is permissible). Donations may be made ONLY by American citizens.

Section 4: Political Action Committees (PAC) (business entities may not contribute to candidates or coordinate their activities with candidates) may be formed by individuals who wish to independently support candidates. There are no restrictions on the amount of funds which a PAC may collect in support of a particular candidate. However, PAC spending for a particular candidate is limited in the same way and to the same dollar amount as a candidate, $1 per registered voter in a district election, state election, or national election. In addition, each PAC must disclose (weekly) publicly the names of its members and how much each member contributed to each candidate. PAC's may not collect funds within 24 days of the election date (or the start of early voting where that applies) and must issue a final PUBLIC disclosure of its membership and individual contribution totals made in support of each candidate no later than 10 days before voting begins. Disclosure must be widely available through the media and the PAC's website.

While there will continue to be an out-of-proportion influence by small groups or those of wealth, at least we will know who is supporting who or what and for what reasons. Only then can we, as American voters, decide who or what we choose to support. Our decisions must not be clouded by the influence of dollar signs. **Citizen's United cannot stand**. Corporations are run by humans; those humans have the right to use their money any way that they see fit, within legal limits, but the immense power and resources of corporations must be limited to producing products and services only! They only exist to create jobs for people and serve the needs of the public!

Investment Banking/Stock Market Trading Rule Changes

Investment banking in this country in 2008 led to one of the worst economic crises since the Stock Market crash of 1929 because of greed. Bundling of strong and weak mortgages to sell them to others was simply a sly (unethical in my opinion) way of dumping what they knew were bad or weak loans. It showed that banking and the stock markets, not just in this country but around the world, are nothing more than casino operations, speculating with the fates of millions of future retirees. The advent of computer trading has made it possible for these "traders" to buy and sell millions of times a minute, taking small profits per share but also collecting fees for trades on both ends, from buyers and from sellers. It's a racket, nothing more.

There is a solution to this, but so long as the "foxes are in charge of the hen house," nothing will be done. Transactions need to be slowed down so that everything is easily transparent. While I can't prove it, I have a sneaking suspicion that some traders are using computers to "buy" stocks that their clients have ordered at one price, raising the price a few cents, and then turning around and delivering the stocks to their clients at the "new price." On top of that, they charge the client a transaction fee. What a racket! Imagine if real estate agents did that! At least they are regulated and only charge a fee to the seller. Of course, the buyer is paying that fee, but the buyer doesn't care because his price is what he has negotiated. If he had to pay a commission on top of the negotiated price, imagine the anger there.

New rules for stock/bond transactions:

1. Commissions are paid by the seller only.

2. Transactions are not complete until funds are transferred and confirmed by both banks. (No kiting of stock/bond purchases. Minimum "cooling off" period of 5 days.)

New IRS rules for stock/bond transactions:

1. All stock/bond transactions are treated as profits or losses for income tax purposes. Capital gains tax differences for short or long term gains and losses are abolished. Income taxes of 10% must be withheld for every transaction to account for social security/national health/income taxes due to potential gains on investments.

2. Stock/bonds must be held for six months before they can be sold. (This will significantly put a dent in speculating on stocks/bonds)

3. Day Trading is abolished.

4. Selling short is abolished.

You have to wonder how much fraud would exist if these simple rules were in place! The other area of great concern is commodity sales. Speculation in commodities has driven the price of many goods through the roof in this country and around the world. It's time to end some of this. I would suggest the following:

Commodities can only be sold by producers to direct users.

(**Example 1**: wheat can only be sold to mills for processing. They, in turn, can only sell to manufacturers who actually use the processed wheat in foods.)

(**Example 2**: oil can only be sold by production companies to refineries. They, in turn, can only sell to companies who use the petroleum products in their manufacturing processes or distribute directly to consumers.) "Middle men" who only buy and sell as speculators should be outlawed. It only drives up the prices of end products.

Commodity exchanges should be banned in so far as food and fuel are concerned. While some minerals probably belong on that list, I will leave that to those who know more about this than I do.

A final proposal is to return to stricter regulation of banks and other financial institutions. Stability must be a priority. Credit availability and abuse by both borrowers and lenders has gotten out of hand and should be better controlled. **Interest rates must be fixed according to law-PERIOD!** My belief is that banks should only be allowed to charge Six Percent APR, though that is negotiable. Fees and charges must be closely monitored and approved before banks can change them. **All customers should be equal and subject to those charges. Whether rich or poor, charges should be the same.**

Credit cards should have a set maximum interest rate of Eight Percent APR, though that is negotiable as well. Late Fees must also be fixed and the same for all credit card issuers. Limits should be at the discretion of the card issuers. If the only reason that someone is granted credit is at a higher rate, then that person shouldn't be getting credit, PERIOD! While these changes will not prevent bankruptcy and the kind of financial instability which has so damaged the economy of this country, they will go a long way to eventually put us back on an even keel. The financial well-being of not only this country but the entire planet should not be left to the whims of the wealthy or the "gamblers" among us who would rather make money at the expense of others. When someone makes a "gain" on the sale of a stock, someone else is "losing." My suggestion is "get a regular job and work hard like most people do." Go to a regular casino if you want to risk your savings. Buy antiques and speculate that way. Buy an old house, renovate it, and resell it at a profit. That is a decent way to increase your savings. Stocks and bonds were never meant to be a medium for gamblers. They were a means for a company to acquire cash to invest in a business which hires people, creates needed products, and supports this country.

Prison/Law/Court Reform

Our criminal justice system must be reformed. I once heard someone make the following statement (or something to the effect): **"There are two reasons to put people in prison. There are those who we fear and those who we wish to punish."** Of course, many prisoners fit both categories, but there is a difference. The populations of our prisons should be divided in just this way. Who do we fear? Violence cannot be tolerated in a civilized society (which we claim to be), so those who physically, and, to some extent, mentally injure others, whether during the commission of some crime or not, should be housed among those of a similar inclination. Perhaps in some cases their violent natures may be changed (that's for psychiatrists to determine), but these criminals must not be allowed to spread their violent mentality among those who aren't. I have long believed that these inmates should be kept in single cells with access to "exercise periods" without physical contact with others. It might require building new facilities for violent inmates. If it protects guards and other inmates, then it's the right thing to do. They would still have both visual and conversational contact with their fellow inmates, but no physical contact would be allowed. By doing this, injuries in these prisons would be nearly non-existent. Whatever counseling and medication that would be deemed appropriate could be handled in a safe and humane manner.

Perhaps it's also time to think about life sentences for these offenders, if they aren't already sentenced to life. The alternative, to me, is for these types of people to be exiled to a "colony" which could be created in a remote area or on an island, where they could have more freedom and have a more normal chance to live out their days. I'm open to suggestions. I also believe that any prisoner who receives a life sentence should be given the option of "death" at any time. **I am opposed to the death penalty for the simple reason that our experience during the past years has shown us that not everyone sentenced to death is actually guilty**. Our courts and juries do their best, but should we really be putting people to death? Who do we want to punish? There are plenty of non-violent offenders who deserve what they get. Robbery, drug dealing, kidnapping, white-collar crime (remember Bernie Madoff, not to mention the thousands of corporate CEO's who deserve to be held liable for the damage that their companies have created), and the many other crimes for which we incarcerate individuals are reasons to punish, but we don't normally fear for our safety, only our finances.

I believe that more judges should utilize "creative, more appropriate" sentences, ones which help to pay the victims rather than just cost the taxpayers to provide room and board and medical care to someone for years. We now have the capability to electronically monitor criminals, thus making it possible to confine them without the expense of a prison cell. Let their families pay their expenses. Let them go to work and reimburse their victims and society in a financial manner. While I know that this doesn't fit every individual, it should be used more often than it is at present.

The trend has been and appears to be returning to using "private" prison facilities. I oppose this because, in the long run, it will be more expensive and require more prison inmates and for longer sentences so that the private prisons can show a profit. They won't stay open if we don't keep them at a capacity which allows them to so. I see that as ripe for corruption and fraud. While the U.S. has approximately 5% of the world's population, we have nearly 25% of the world's prison population. Of course, the law enforcement and court systems in our part of the world are more efficient and better enforced, but it also speaks to a larger problem, drugs.

Before the current version of the "war on drugs" (1980, more or less), about 150 people per 100,000 population were in prison. Several years ago that figure was about 750 per 100,000. That's between 5 and 10 TIMES MORE than other "modern countries."

More than half of all inmates in this country are there on drug-related convictions. They're not all "dealers;" as much as 80% of those are possession charges, not the big boys! The war on drugs has failed; just ask any state with an "opioid epidemic" such as Vermont or New Hampshire or West Virginia! Prison is the right place for drug dealers, but users who need and want help should be able to get it. Time in treatment facilities would be cheaper than prison. Some states spend over $10,000 a year per inmate. Doesn't it make sense to at least try to help medically before wasting that money on prison? If a five-year sentence costs us $50,000, why not spend

$25,000 on a long-term treatment program to at least try to end a person's addiction?

How do we really fight the drug problem? When it comes to heroin or cocaine or other drugs which originate outside of the U.S. and are imported, we should go to the source and stop production, whatever it takes. A more proactive approach, which should be with the cooperation of whatever country it involves, should involve the use of our military, whether special forces or regular forces. Destroying production facilities, over and over again if necessary, along with either arresting/prosecuting the bosses and workers or, if necessary, eliminating them altogether is the only way to prevent the production before the drugs are in the pipeline. In so far as the domestic production of drugs, such as meth and artificial hallucinogenics, law enforcement must continue to seek out and destroy those production facilities as well, using whatever means necessary.

Marijuana, however, is another story. "Pot" may or may not be worse than alcohol, but it is here and will never be eliminated. It has medicinal value, whether the "powers that be" in Washington want to believe it or not. Marijuana should be legalized with the same restrictions as alcohol and met with the same punishments for violations. Is it harmful? Absolutely, if abused in the same way that alcohol can be abused. It should be regulated, monitored by the Agriculture Department for purity, and regulated by A.T.F., just as cigarettes are now. The tax revenue alone would be a boost to the health industry if that tax money were directed to a national health insurance program, just as the alcohol tax should be. With drug offenders out of the prison system, we could concentrate on protecting people from those who are violent by isolating them where they can do no more harm and punishing those who have preyed on honest citizens. Our system is broken, but it can be fixed. Citizens must force Congress to listen and do what makes sense!

Gun Ownership Rights and Responsibilities

Let there be no misunderstanding; **I fully support and defend the right of Americans to own/carry and use properly (according to state and local laws) both handguns and rifles/shotguns.** That being said, I believe that there needs to be a change in the laws regarding military-style weapons and high-capacity magazines, PERIOD! The original intent of the founding fathers was to guarantee that states would have a "militia" (National Guard now) was a reaction to the historical period when the goal was to prevent our young nation from being defenseless in case of an invasion by England. That threat was real as England did attack America in 1812. Had we not had these "militias," it is possible that this country would have fallen to England. That threat no longer exists, but the need is there for each state to have a military-style unit for emergencies. They are used frequently across the country to help in weather-related emergencies or to help when small groups attempt to usurp the power of the state legislature.

The intent was never for each man, woman, and child to be a walking soldier. It is easily demonstrated that the rest of the "truly civilized world" doesn't feel the need for guns in every home. Our tradition of the "old west" still lives within the DNA of many Americans, as it should be when it comes to national security. However, fair and reasonable attempts to regulate the weapon industry and those who seek to use them for purposes other than legal must be allowed. Laws which encourage safety should be urged by organizations such as the NRA. However, they have shirked their responsibility in that area and created an atmosphere of distrust. I would never seek to remove handguns, rifles and shotguns from the homes of hunters, competitors, or collectors who are responsible, safe gun owners.

Handguns and military-style weapons, on the other hand, need to be closely regulated. It would be easier and more effective if the NRA and other such organizations would work with legislatures to write laws to do that. The harder decision has to do with "who should not have a weapon of any kind." While I don't have the answer, we must work together as responsible citizens to find a way to keep weapons out of the hands of those who are not responsible, who have mental illnesses, and who have a history of violence. There has to be a way to write such laws so that people's rights are protected but so are innocent citizens who more and more are becoming victims of senseless gun violence. **"No man was ever endowed with a right without being at the same time saddled with a responsibility!" (Gerald W. Johnson: Saturday Review, July 5, 1958)**

This is a Global Economy!

Like it or Not, we live in a world WITH a Global Economy That statement begs the question, "How does the United States 1) increase good-paying, sustainable jobs for American citizens, 2) sell products in foreign countries, not just here at home, 3) use trade as a way to improve the world's environmental issues, 4) help foreign workers improve their wages and working conditions, and 5) correct our balance-of-payments deficit?

It cannot simply be about more American jobs and profits! Left to the corporate CEO's, whose salaries and bonuses are based on their company profits, the future (which is how we got to where we are now) is merely an afterthought for the short-sighted. Few care about anything beyond their "bottom line." Certainly the more important concern for American policy makers should be American jobs. They are the ones who vote, right? However, every trade deal must begin with the understanding that there are two sides to every negotiation. There must be incentives on both sides for a workable deal to be reached. U.S. companies don't want foreign products coming into the country which undercut their sales and profits. The auto industry hated the idea of the Japanese car makers invading their space with smaller, more efficient vehicles, especially ones that were cheaper. The cry was "Buy American! You're UN-American if you buy a foreign car!" Many people did just that, but enough saw that it was economically smarter to buy foreign. It took "Detroit" a few years to get the point. Better, cheaper, more fuel-efficient cars began to be built in the U.S. that were competitive.

Eventually, foreign companies began to manufacture here in the U.S. The competition created a better industry! Everybody won! That being said, if the products had been of the same quality, then a tariff should have been imposed which brought the price 64 of those foreign vehicles up to the equivalent American model. That would have been fair. Today, if Maytag wants to sell the same model washer in the U.S. that it makes in Mexico, then its price should not be lower than an American equivalent model. (Of course, I believe that those companies who leave to find cheaper costs overseas should be required to repay all local, state, and federal "tax benefits, etc." that they received which they used to create the business at the start. That's only fair!

However, some companies left the U.S. just because of the cheaper labor elsewhere. This problem actually provides an opportunity to attack several problems at once. If X Company has moved to, say, Mexico, to produce the same product much lower and then shipping it back to the U.S., the solution is a "floating tariff." By this I mean a tariff which keeps the price no higher than the equivalent American-made product. The difference in price goes into a fund for displaced workers. This tariff can be reduced by the importing manufacturer in several ways. First, it must increase the wages of its workers, bring up their standard of living. Second, it must increase its investment in cleaning up its corporate environment (waste disposal, reducing air pollution, reducing its carbon footprint in numerous ways). These will increase the cost of its product and put it on a more level selling field with the American product which is already doing those things, which keeps its cost high. At this point, the two products can be sold in either country for basically the same price. The better product will always sell more. The incentive is to improve products. This sort of tariff approach helps balance the import/export balance of payments.

Trade opportunities should be open across all borders, giving the United States the same opportunity for sales as it does other countries. One product in particular that has been in recent news is Harley Davidson, a world leader in motorcycle production. Apparently their products are subject to heavy tariffs in certain countries. If they want to sell their motorcycles in the United States, those foreign producers should be subject to tariffs here until it's a level field. Perhaps their workers should be making better wages or the companies could be doing more to improve the global environment? Trade could be the most powerful tool that we have to lead the world's environmental cleanup. Everyone wants to sell products in the United States. If they will improve the lives of their workers and clean up the air, water, and soil, their costs will be the same as ours. We share the planet, so we have to share the cost of saving it! Trade, jobs, and the environment must go hand-in-hand.

Editorials:

NO Major Religious Doctrine Teaches HATE! My personal philosophy is fairly simple: "I have the right to believe and do whatever I want so long as it doesn't interfere with the right of someone else to believe or do whatever he/she wants!" I have read the Bible, the Quran, the Torah, and many of the books of the other major philosophies (religion is a personal philosophy, NOT a part of a person's DNA). The largest six religious doctrines in the world today are Christianity (2 billion followers), Islam (1.2 billion), Hinduism (820 million), Buddhism (362 million), Judaism (14.5 million), and Confucianism (6.3 million). NONE of the mainstream groups of these philosophies teach hatred, violence, or discrimination. It is only individuals who associate themselves with various philosophies who resort to 81 hatred, violence, or discrimination, either out of ignorance or frustration that others don't believe as they do. When politicians or public figures endorse policies to discriminate, to denigrate, or to encourage others to resort to violence or hate speech, they do nothing to solve problems. If it's a way to get votes, that's a sorry way to win an election or gain support for whatever issue you endorse. The only people who respond positively to negative ads or speeches which spread hate or encourage discrimination or outright violence belong to one of several groups: ignorant, uneducated, uninformed, mentally ill, or criminal. If there were one, true religion, then humans would be born with that belief, just as humans automatically breathe and eat/drink to survive.

Religion/philosophy is a CHOICE. My choice is my choice; your choice is your choice. Neither of us has THE answer unless it is to respect each others choice. If you don't like another religion/philosophy, don't associate with it or its members. However, DOING something negative is NOT YOUR RIGHT; you don't have the right to keep anyone else from making a choice

The lack of civility in our public discourse must change!

As I listen to not only politicians, who should be setting the standard, but also to average people, it is apparent that our society has lost the ability to disagree without screaming or insulting one another. Unfortunately, this has led to bullying, insulting, and violence. Demonizing other people, calling them evil or hateful, serves no purpose. It only creates anger and hurt, which serves no purpose. Rather than calling some a liar, why not explain the fallacy in the rhetoric or error in the facts. I see it at political rallies, online in Facebook videos, on the television news, and often as I shop at local stores. It must stop! If you want someone to hear your point of view, you must be willing to listen to his/her viewpoint as well. Only uneducated or ignorant or fanatics speak using vulgar, hateful language because they don't understand that doing that doesn't advance their point of view. It is only by sitting down, explaining why you support a particular position with facts or "beliefs" and then listening as the other person does the same. The two of you can then examine the facts, calmly discuss the issue, and, at least, understand each other that you can either compromise or, at the very least, accept that the other person won't cede to your point of view.

Emotional frustration does nothing to further public discourse. If this country is to survive, if the violence between people over political issues is to end, we must agree to disagree, without the hateful words or accusations. Isn't it better to leave your opponent with "food for thought" than a bruised ego or heavy heart? Many times there is a "middle ground" where both sides can have a small victory! "The individual who persecutes a man, his brother, because he is not of the same opinion, is a monster!"(Voltaire: Philosophical Dictionary, 1764; miscellaneous) So long as we refuse to listen to others opinions and refuse to examine them, discuss them rationally and calmly, we will remain "monsters." It is only through "civil discourse" that America can thrive and build a unified future. None of us have all the answers!

The True "Enemy of the People is a lie!"

Investigative journalism is defined as follows: **"Reporting, through one's own initiative and work product, matters of importance to readers, viewers or listeners." (University of Missouri journalism professor Steve Weinberg).** In many cases, the subjects of the reporting wish the matters under scrutiny to remain undisclosed. **"An investigative journalist is a man or woman whose profession it is to discover the truth and to identify lapses from it in whatever media may be available. The act of doing this generally is called investigative journalism and is distinct from apparently similar work done by police, lawyers, auditors and regulatory bodies in that it is not limited as to target, not legally founded and closely connected to publicity. (British media theorist Hugo de Burgh (2000))** **(http://dictionary.sensagent.com/Investigative_journalism/en-en/)**

For some time now, journalism, not just investigative journalism, has been under attack in this country, not to mention around the world. A politician, any public servant, gives up the right to "secrecy and privacy" in public service matters when they take the oath of office. All elected officials are constantly scrutinized by the 4th Estate, our Free Press. Anyone who can't handle that has no place in public service. The Free Press has not only the right but also the RESPONSIBILITY to shine a light on everything that our elected/appointed/hired officials do and say in our name. The media is NOT of ENEMY OF THE PEOPLE! These men and women risk their lives every day to protect us from anyone who would lie, cheat, and steal while in our service. They are the heroes of democracy! The only ones who despise them are those who have something to hide or who do not understand the critical value and importance of a Free Press! Perhaps they don't belong in office!

"The last right we shall mention, regards the freedom of the press. The importance of this consists, besides the advancement of truth, science, morality, and arts in general, in its diffusion of liberal sentiments on the administration of Government, its ready communication of thoughts between subjects, and its consequential promotion of union among them, whereby oppressive officials are shamed or intimidated, into more honorable and just modes of conducting affairs." (Continental Congress: Letter to the inhabitants of Quebec, 1774; quoted by Justice Brennan, Roth v. U.S., U.S. 476 (1957).

After thoughts...

We may be members of different political parties, if members of any at all, but our futures and the future of this "experiment" in citizen leadership "of the people, by the people, and for the people" hinges on our belief that we should be led by good, decent, compassionate representatives to Congress and a President who tries to represent all Americans, not just those who provide financially support.

Every registered voter should go to the polls this November. THIS election is more important than the last one was.

PLEASE VOTE!!!

www.ingramcontent.com/pod-product-compliance
Lightning Source LLC
Chambersburg PA
CBHW070435290526
45791CB00005B/1979